Winner of the
2009 Omnidawn Poetry Prize

The Madeleine Poems

The Madeleine Poems

PAUL LEGAULT

OMNIDAWN PUBLISHING

RICHMOND, CALIFORNIA

2010

Cover Art: "Tada" by Becca Durnin
Cover Design and Author Photo: Billy Merrell

Typefaces: Adobe Jenson Pro and Adobe Kabel LT

Offset printed in the United States on archival, acid-free recycled paper
by Thomson-Shore, Inc., Dexter, Michigan

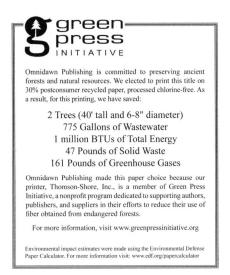

green press
INITIATIVE

Omnidawn Publishing is committed to preserving ancient forests and natural resources. We elected to print this title on 30% postconsumer recycled paper, processed chlorine-free. As a result, for this printing, we have saved:

2 Trees (40' tall and 6-8" diameter)
775 Gallons of Wastewater
1 million BTUs of Total Energy
47 Pounds of Solid Waste
161 Pounds of Greenhouse Gases

Omnidawn Publishing made this paper choice because our printer, Thomson-Shore, Inc., is a member of Green Press Initiative, a nonprofit program dedicated to supporting authors, publishers, and suppliers in their efforts to reduce their use of fiber obtained from endangered forests.

For more information, visit www.greenpressinitiative.org

Environmental impact estimates were made using the Environmental Defense Paper Calculator. For more information visit: www.edf.org/papercalculator

Library of Congress Catalog-in-Publication Data

Legault, Paul, 1985-
    The Madeleine poems / Paul Legault.
       p. cm.
    ISBN 978-1-890650-48-3 (pbk. : alk. paper)
    I. Title.
    PS3612.E3516M33 2010
    811'.6--dc22
                                            2010030934

Published by Omnidawn Publishing, Richmond, California
www.omnidawn.com   (510) 237-5472   (800) 792-4957
       10 9 8 7 6 5 4 3 2 1
          ISBN: 978-1-890650-48-3

ACKNOWLEDGEMENTS

My thanks to the following publications where some of these poems have previously appeared: *Burnside Review, Denver Quarterly, Drunken Boat, FIELD, Interim, Pistola, Pleiades.*

CONTENTS

For my husband Orion.
And for Madeleine.

Many of us go farther. My pathetic Crusoe -

Emily Dickinson

MADELEINE

Open *The Book of Take* and leave
open the book of your arrival.

    Call me the Madonna of chosen things.
  Know I am righteous and moth-like.

Wash me or tear me; knead me in lye;
 know then that I will outlast you.

  That it was hot,
the houses burnt down;
  the way of fire even in spring then.

      Woodsnail, breathe for me,
  or beware your life
  which I will take and shudder just to hold it.

Everyone was rich.
  We hunted wild animals.
The worst was when they looked at you.

MADELEINE AS THE HOMOSEXUALS

They have not lost each other as we will expect them to.

These were their names: Paul, Gabriel, or Lance.

I would say no to a long car ride, unless there were boys in the car, and we were in
   love with each other, and we were going somewhere nice, and Lance was driving,
   and I could drink whiskey.
But I would go for any reason if it was June and we were going.

> My grandmother's name is a field where men stop their bicycles
> on the premise that there will be a luncheon—

> *Madeleine—*

> —and get sucked off for the first time
> romantically in fields.

Let us ask them about the life of the city.
   Let us ask them have they been born again.

Or have they a language
or a symbol for the homosexual's eventual reincarnation.

Or their song:
> *Take away*
> *This animal*
> *Death. Let us*
> *To the death of plants.*

> They have
> fished and lived at the edge of a gulf, there at the dip of

salt into water. This was
the place of them.

> They were
> there before it—passage

> to chestnut, passage to
> the dark anatomy.

MADELEINE AS THE BALLOON AND SIZE FROM HERE

*

Whiteward: this first direction.

*

Sometimes, in her drunken navigation, she'd admire the elegant shape of a bottle emptying inches past the basket.

*

Must over France, must over even the idea of trace—windowless, sand-met, glassing…

*

The bird stepped into yellow as if in a war. The farms as if in a war. These days turned golden in their meat as if…

*

Everything quickly became penultimate—the feeling, not the act of some yet-to-be-had arrival.

*

I wish I was a mole in the ground. Not this riding to the north—measured by an impeccable compass.

*

The first birds blacken. The farthest gulls. Little knots that couldn't be tied to.

*

Sometimes a buffalo stands in the open, wanting his good buffalo.

*

I wish I was a lizard in the spring. If I's a lizard in the spring, then I'd hear my darling sing.

*

Or a thought breaks in the arctic. Or does not. We are too much of us.

MADELEINE AS JAMES DEAN AND THE WHALE

The whale holds its blue saw against
　　　　the Pacific drift.
Wish to be a held thing, whale.

How many knots was it
tightened to make you,
　　　　pulled to the pull
in the water—against, and you against it, and the water, and sounding—

　　　　WHALE: (*breathlessly*) I affirm me.
　　　　WHALE'S-HEART: (*the size of a train compartment*) WOOMP.

　　　　WHALE: Well, what did you expect from a whale's heart?
　　　　JAMES DEAN: (*his face pressed to the compartment-window*) The
　　　　　　strange replies. And the phrase: 'stone-wash' repeated. Not like
　　　　　　the jeans but like the body of a whale. Not with a strict meaning
　　　　　　either. Or meaning that it makes the thing live.

It is not your newness anymore.
Ride from it—the city rides from it.

It is not into
that the breath goes.
　　　　Search the blind earth for the blind earth.

Rarest of histories, the contemporary history
is a yeti, is a taken yeti—taken

　　　　in a patrol car, into a keeping
of things which was only a keeping
　　　　of things which were wild there once.

　　　　Once of the day, twice of the night,
James Dean, release your glorious cock.

Blue under. Blue in. I go out.
        Sometimes the wreckages

leave off for
        disobedience, the right to
leave off from
this whale-life
(in this whale-body (in this whale-place… (in…

MADELEINE AS TRAVELOGUE

Then to the island, Madeleine.
Then to the Bridgeport masses.
Then to the unmined
      animal quarries of

          that that is rock from us
          that arranges

us and all these Madeleines,
all these bones without—
all this length of blue colonnade with,

then without—then to the moon's stunted architectures.
Then to be brought to this.

Then a Madeleine, then a poor source of—
      Then a Madeleine, my marchioness.

Imponderable corollaries—the streams that carry gold.
O, my miner, mine these
      animal quarries of

          that that tries rock
          that is stone without—you

do not speak but undress
all the public spaces.

First all the brooches. Rifle through
the pockets for each passport.

They have no need. There is none.
Then to the foreigners' country without—
      No, to go on is against us.

MADELEINE AS TRAVELOGUE

No, grass widow.
No, grass widow. Go from it—

    your living in countries,
                horses,

and the new flags of the spring-
                embroideries—sewn into these

     flawless exits,
        one imagines the hem;

          the open face of
          the house with no overhang. The door in the brick. Say so,
    ugly house:

Leave. It is such that its first things went.
The mirrors placed flat on the lawn. The movers sleeping. The grass caught
   above them stirred. The grass stirs. Stirred little green knives. Stirred
      little thieves—the little bones in their faces. Move from them,
   clockmaker. The thieves. And their little sister-assistants. Madeleine,
there is no one with each of the small bones of his face for you.

MADELEINE AS HOME

*

In one of the rooms, time gets really close.

*

One room is for the dog. There is either a large pillow or a small bed in this room. The dog is expected to die in this room. Eventually, the dog will probably die in this room.

*

This is the room in which you wake up. It is different from the room in which you'd gone to sleep. In this room there is always a mirror in which your face appears to be moving. Your face is not necessarily moving. This can be a disconcerting room.

*

This room with the dolphins is not entirely unpleasant. It is very wet. If you have things in your pockets, you should've already removed them. The dolphins' pockets' contents are hidden.

*

This is the room with the new dinette set.

*

In one of the rooms there are many wonderful big hats. In this room, everyone is wearing wonderful big hats, and if you are not wearing one, I will get you one, and you will wear it in this room with the rest of them.

*

In the orange room, the roses do not die unless you are looking.

*

In the next room, the chifforobe is to be called 'the chifforobe.'

*

In one of the rooms, a person has just arrived. It is then that the room has become something. Before then, there had been perhaps the idea of space, and a dark shuffling somewhere deep in the furniture, a stillness which is a thing, or which can be, though it was only then that you noticed it, the stillness then with the person in the room that made it a place, and if not a permanent place, then all the more a place for the transitive nature of it, like a music.

MADELEINE AS FIRE-WATCH

Somnambulist, no more of long walks with you.
What then? What
        else but long walks with the somnambulist?
           Then a new accompaniment;
a green station to which we are drafted
        out to the wilderness for
a day, then a day, then
        a day only
—things do not
accumulate
at this post.
           Master me! O
the trees' coquettish opera!

MADELEINE AS MATADOR

The last kerchief—
that was your Spanish

dress, Malaga, under it,
your doll's feet
            that scurried to blood.

Then there was no body but a garment.
Then you are naked in the day's corridors.
            I am a tassel. Do

beware me.

MADELEINE AS YEOMAN

Free down to the caskets
        hurried the leashmen. Set to

ride, I am, set to
        ride, Sally. Many a man dead,
few set to ride. Tie the good rope
to a good beast—Atlantica.
It is less about accuracy as myth.
        Use a square knot
        and the winter's cable.
Name a season 'Sally,' and it smiles.

        I were a man, I'd call you a woman.
I were a woman, you're mine.

MADELEINE AS LICE

Not to speak—let the whole in.
Let this be the job of small things.

I have some stolen reliquaries
that bunk the dark. I have

a mouth for the dog's life.
Host me to this—
it was that that was

and was left to what
it was and was not
what we think of it.

MADELEINE AS MATHEMATICIAN

The integration of language and music was difficult until the word *arithmetic*. Different systems yield the same result. Mine is chronological. I could leave or stay and time would prove me.

MADELEINE AS PORNOGRAPHER

Let there be trees more than prostitutes, but let them both be.
Let the wing be without and within.

There is a visible pinning and one under. There is a coffer and a barrel
    and a rope braided from iron.
There were three men before one, and they came to each other in the baths.
That each was kind to their lambs'-bodies and gentle in the removal of socks.
That there is no name for the sea's need but need, and none for the expansion
    thereof.
Let Chance mark on paper as well as it has the moving edges of these gods
    of American sport—each who is measured daily by the breadth of an
    earlobe, or by his height when asleep, or by the short distances of his
    pigments' constellations that shift: by north, by east, each by the man's
    compass, and seek the future astrologically, and speak it.

MADELEINE AS TOURIST

Boys in shorts
   will be the death of me.
     Here and always Sunday,

I cannot help if I rise of God—
   or act a parliament to
their secretaryship.

Boys in farm life, etc.,
   and of the gravemaker down Grand.
   I have left business

up to the dead—the dead without
   their businesses, their deaths of them, their boys
for example, or lives.

Oh, why not make us this
   nothing we have for us
   a hell to come to?

This is where a love is starting: you.
I think that we should be tequila
     and let heaven be

the pity we've made.
     You buy the white horse
just to sell it back.

   Tuft of fur at your throat,
tuft at your belly
below where each breath that you swallow goes.

MADELEINE AS SISTER

Recall yourself, simple disaster.
The world is all that's needed.

You were given these images at birth,
then who can call them otherworldly?

Strike them from your body,
the frail-lipped porpoises. Warn the light

to show them no longer,
magenta, whose queen is called Arabelle.

Were they to speak we could give them a species.
These are the creatures of silence.

Let them. Let them say in the open,
given the chance, they would die for it.

MADELEINE AS HEROINE

Take your life.
The hour precludes it—and the nights' week.
The heart—I think it made of skin—
the fist—that a day brings to it—

swallows and six-sided things, or else
the shapeful poppies—all these
red cogs that turn the blood—all these were.

One would give it—it being
it all—one would gladly siphon
all of one to say
I have watched her seal an envelope.

Or worse, I have seen her
take three paces back from me,
reach to a door in the air,
step into her invisible plane and then nothing.

MADELEINE AS PORTRAIT OF WALT WHITMAN AS GERTRUDE STEIN AS A STRIPPER

You bright slut.
The hard harden; the soft
exchange their billowing roses
and play out the dead
and rhymed and country melodies, lovely—
but to men, but to women; but for gloss
and switch of sex, they were the same
name to call to, ignoble godheads, all of us. Some debut.

We have given you—
we are each of us
goodnesses, little lives of heavy
cost, wing, and gravity
—your audience. O, centripetal force, O, fugue
of poor lighting, of disco ball stewards. Swing
hard down with a horror of height
and the midriff astrain with leaning of—low for them—this your body.

Daffodil, do not
look past your looks
which are yours as they are yours to wed to
whom you will—
the son or the mother, the proud nationalist, the kid
you had without border. This is your mouth. This
is not your city. This nakedness
is yours but not this day—though it exists for no one else.

Who never aspired
to be a word that meant
secretly Maverick, loose knot, drawn
string, and god all at once?
There's no such name, but you come close,
dark swaggerer. I have seen you over-and
-overing. Render each beatitude
useless. Make us enough for us, beautiful soldier. The hungry

will be filled,
the ready given arms.
All the living must know you by now.
You have let them.

MADELEINE AS STONE, WHAT IS TO DIE OF YOU?

Dolls seldom have teeth. Still, I want a doll's tooth
for my wedding ring. After all, it is my birthstone.

MADELEINE AS THE NEW FRONTIER

We had no name for it.
The trouble's mine.
Arthur.

A lady in each lake,
each lake a wide apostle,
no fish but a lady
as a fish or a sword.

King bring kindling
to the pyre, the lit man
losing ground.

Or who am I and where are we
in the November of December?
Shoot you, bird, you
bow & sparrow,
lightly. Or to a fist.

    *

Wings and water.
The settlement of a body.
And the settlers.

There are places with no men
or women traveling there
that dare the animal.

This Newfoundland.
Hold me, Leif Ericson.

All of your body
in Jellyfish Cove.

Leif of a blood tradition,

sail the flat rock flat,

red Leif,
maybe this is a war of bridles.

*

Blue keep.
Columbus.
How much heaven we are given.

Send out these
like bodies to
like bodies or
else to those foreign
bodies of water

which he described to Isabella: the world

as a pear with a nipple on top

that she would imagine exploration always

as such an odd breast as the Earth
in a red box, opened on no great day,

a gift, a nipple and pear
for the queen to mouth in Castile.

*

Daniel Boone.
I imagine a vast hat.

Coonskin bed.
Lay me down into it.

Bird, you, bird,
appear as sharp as water.

There are only so many deaths.

MADELEINE AS WHITE COUNTRY

At least
you can sleep by
the American names for loneliness:
Iowa, Nebraska, Memphis, like snow
that we had to talk about
when it refused to go away.
Give it names,
names for names' sake:
ashes, the winter, the white earth.

To build a man up from it
is to want for him
to rid us from what he is made of
by leaving on a horse of snow

into spring, even now.
The land exists. Ruin.
Snow. He will stay.
The patterns of milk, of place

like a fluid, snowmen that know nothing
of competition, of men made
of red and not water,
of blood that keeps through summer.

You may as well make him a home by now
from snow and a wife
of sorts from snow and a mouth,
because they will make a name for themselves
from snow and the means to wait
from ice, from carrots and coal,
their wide language derived from the weather
without a single word for you,
ten for the sea,
nothing for the cold.

MADELEINE AS IDITAROD

Dog, watch your ghost in the milk bowl;
I saw that it was like mine when it bent over
to the high wind.
You smell through its cold dress;
the hem is a whore's hem.
Feed no ghost.
Show me where
you found the stunt flag of its dream.

The wheatdog
hid his bone in an oven.
We learned to make bread.

The whiskeydog
made us cry, he crawled into a barrel
to close his sweet life like a book
or a good drink
on the house, for the thirsty ghost.

Tell me about your wants like a woman;
they are the justification of sound.
Do not shrug
or claim you are not the Lady Macbeth
who follows me out late to pee in the snow.
You are the lead dog
of rush, the king of our wood and our stone.
Love can mean speed.
We began a new race.

MADELEINE AS FOREST GOSPEL

Heather,
know this heated room was left your brother.
Moondog,
I'm sure we'll meet again in yonder minefields.
Mother,
shake this tarry cloth above your shoulder
and mend me, mother, mend me.

Black moose, it is
a private thing.

Black moose, black
moose, your wings are widely
outstretched and foreign to the jackdaw.

They seem to be of wood but are of bone
and made to spear the air. No wounded bird,

You are a moose, tremendous
moose. And dying of a slowness in the blood.

MADELEINE AS ODE OF A NIGHTINGALE

I had an art, and it was mine. The little
songs or voices—these
        portions of a life's happiness—

      if we had two it was only
to stave off the crowds who'd watch us

through a glass or else were
   lumbering, only an ax
to their names (O the secrets

objects share). The screams of a grasshopper—
those were their lives—
   those that hated birds' nests

      (our very battlements
      (our parapets (or crestings)
of crenels; (crenellation…)))

     Wind, wind, wind-wind,
fine and corpulent…to the rafters   we hid in…

        Wind when wilt…
the small rain down
   shall rain O Christ,
     O Western,
O
     John James
Audubon, what we had was always a danger.

MADELEINE AS SUPPLY

All the early distances are buried

distances, all the early
   systems were systems

   of measurement, what use
have we, for what we have

here is a list of our weekly duties,
and one must learn to live negligent

of—or else to breathe
           for these strange youths
cornered on a sailboat only
           by sea and shore and a civic pride—
Jacob and his scholar ride

   —these seas about, these men

about; O, breathe, O, shore,
           what long, ridden passage
of land is this land of old kings

of India, gaslight
empire—we were
asleep and asleep in our languages.

MADELEINE AS CRUSOE

*

May others come to it better than

I have done.
What I have done consists in the world

of what it consists in the world as—
the totality of and as
the totality of—

spring the season of combination, the blood-
birds symbolic of an Earthward-
ness, even Kansas becomes the opening out of

—what betterness they may come to.

*

A thing is in itself—
to name is to bring death to
—eulogy enough.

*

Then to be measured

by division is not to be
ordered to
an ordered default

that we enter at
every coordinate. There must be a common

thing to strive for
as for a system

of limits. There must not be in

order a single
thing of us.

*

It shows it forth—both

the possibility of non-
existence and logic, at once the two

of them that can depict this
wide menagerie of things and of pictures

and of pictures of things: yes or no,

yes or no, yes or no, yes—
burgundy.

*

We live by

primitive means, are given by
every description, and only by placing—

men bound for Berlin and for
other men or bound

for the women who contained them
or did not—as in a thing

that was a life or could be or was
a life of things—
or bound for better

places of little places—the highways of
Lisbon, the green cordage

of Susquehanna or the deepness of

—our utterances
does a name have a meaning

to call to and let arrive.

*

They then signify and are—

as green is green and was—

to exist and to go—being how they were
brought to coloredness

in such a form which was
a language

—and to exclude all errors which
were ours and were not
theirs or things we kept

as if to find in them purpose
as over a treeline or as in these
methods of symbolizing—

a plane out of which gasps a woman.

*

The use of confusion—
and every thing of which it gives

a layer to—a band of bears,
a maze of
concentric hedgerows, what we were

then, dressed in
skivvies and fascinated by

possession—and if it was not
used, it would be left
without even an accidental

meaning—meaning by that
the things we presupposed
ought to enable us a sense of

the commonality in which we
contracted this need for

necessariness.

*

Something else must be the case—

something in which we were
the case of the translation—this

which all have
as though it could be

a thought to have thought of it
at all if it were unthinkable—

a shield of bees—to think of

a case in which
it were not the case in the logical
place—in that each is

the possibility of existence.

*

Take a sign
like *paradise*—every little bird

atop its very own
tree in paradise—and be

given by it.

*

The fields must be explained to us

if we are to understand them—

written prairie, dead or alive—
the crescent beetles living under

a poppy—and the connection is
what it was all along—

a new sense to us

of an old thing, a new
thing of an old thing made

anew—put together of what

was once taken apart,
as it were, for the sake

of experiment—when one name
could somehow answer through

it all to every question.

*

We should be able
to place ourselves—from

within through the unthinkable—
out of the world of us

where we were led by

a deviation—the sound of
a false hen before morning

—in the roads
to the country
that we were bred in
to breed in—

there where the land rises up
by water—again, once

that was us once—

harbourmen, all of us—

quietly sea-delivered.

*

The truth-possibilities of n

are palpably bound
to—with regard to
the agreement of—

boundlessness—and

that they say nothing
is somehow redundant.

*

I know nothing of
the weather when I know

that it rains or does not—

the girls accompanied with gold
umbrellas, the boys caught off-

guard in it—and the ones caught
that know whether—

regarding the arrows of two

men or women in parting—

such or such is the case.

*

What was not
and what—the bell-eyed-horse

horse-carts of—was was only
—which the mere look of which

—not once—meant
a music even to—then it was

only once—the dark-
horse—not

only what—or that it was then—or

how it was each of them or was not
in these—the impressions
of places where

we reined in
these days our lives.

*

We cannot give—
or find it in it here—

the number of names—that was
one once or two—logic

precedes us. It is there
before us. It was

what—Warrior State—
how—the limits of—

Calico—and the fatted
seraphim—
our language—black plum—meant or means

this world of things—
this world of which
we cannot say in words of—

this then the limit of
of.

*

We drew in again
into the hollows of a bridge—

little pieces, little and
made of paper or bread—into

the world as we found it

out to be—to be

this that could not be made—
or else to be—in an important

sense—the method of sound to mouth,

or of the world
to an ownership
of it.

*

To see as in a symbol—in it

itself the thing itself—what
went in went out but multiplied

into a proper structure of
a system of yellow branches

or of a red that bears its own

posturing—Washington
blossoms—the moth

went—the paper conferences—

of work to effort—
of these properties—
we built a zero-method

and put each thing into it
and made our nothing

of every chance and element.

*

And in it it
can be found in it—

even the shape of it
which we made—an empty

mouth—of ourselves

and drew the body—
to a point or else
a time-

lessness—in

to meet it.

*

It will not do for us.

I went out
to bury.

Any more of children—

or that it is at all—
or that it ever was
at all at all—
we were

numerous—numerous which meant
at least one—

by that meaning only we were.

And the dead
grew their numbers
from things named Madeleine.

*

That it is is—

to avoid witness—

what the mystical
feeling was then

in a walled room—
to exist as an unspeakable question

is to lose
even doubt—and yet still

these apparitions of the life lived

repulse us from the dead.

*

Two is red; August:

the final number; the thing

is nearby; my brother
is strong;

and the storm then a piece

of coal and we:

not the engine but of
the engine.

*

The ladder discarded
from where we had reached
this braver world rightly—

what discrete logic—there is indeed

the inexpressible—of a thing

that will take us
in or else will
make us up of

us its only
supposition
of our uses—uses

we so had.

ABOUT THE AUTHOR

Paul Legault was born in Ontario and raised in Tennessee. He holds an MFA in Creative Writing from the University of Virginia and a BFA in Screenwriting from the University of Southern California. His poems have been published in *Denver Quarterly*, *FIELD*, *Pleiades*, and other journals. He is currently working on an English-to-English translation of the complete works of Emily Dickinson, part of which has been published as a chapbook, *The Emily Dickinson Reader, Volume 1* (Try and Make, 2009). He is co-editor of the translation journal, *Telephone*. Paul lives with his husband, Orion Jenkins, in Brooklyn, New York, where he works at the Academy of American Poets.